Prayers for Good Times and Bad

Contributing writers:

Nancy Parker Brummett

Christine A. Dallman

Margaret Anne Huffman

Gary Wilde

Publications International, Ltd.

Nancy Parker Brummett is a freelance writer whose work has appeared in numerous publications, including *Virtue Magazine*. She is the author of the books *Walk With Jesus* and *Simply the Savior*.

Christine A. Dallman has contributed to the devotional publication *The Quiet Hour* and is a former editor and columnist for *Sunday Digest* magazine. She is the author of *Daily Devotions for Seniors*, as well as a coauthor of *How to Let God Help You Through Hard Times*.

Margaret Anne Huffman is an award-winning journalist and former lifestyle editor of the *Shelby News*. She has written and contributed to 18 books, including *Simple Wisdom*, *A Moment With God for Mothers*, and *Everyday Prayers for Grandmothers*.

Gary Wilde is a full-time freelance author and editor who has written numerous books and magazine articles on religious and self-help issues. He is the author of *The Promise of Faith* and the coauthor of *Prayers for Life*.

Contents

Talking to God

The fabric of our lives is woven in many textures with myriad threads, and each thread is meaningful and important. "God is in the details," goes a well-known saying, and God wants us to involve him through prayer in the details threading through our daily lives. Regardless of what we may be experiencing, every day we can find inspiration in prayer conversation with God.

Prayer builds a bridge that spans the distance from isolation to awareness of God's presence and availability. Prayer is listening . . . on God's part and ours. A bottomless well from which we can draw, prayer offers strength and light for times of doubt; clarity and guidance during moments of confusion; security for in-between times of change and upheaval; and energy for rebuilding after loss.

Prayers for Good Times and Bad is designed to help you know God. Brief, conversational prayers in everyday language for all circumstances bring you into companionship with a loving, ever-present God. The message in each blessing and prayer is simple: We are not alone.

Readers are invited to explore all the places where this interested and approachable God may be found. For there is no situation that is beyond God's interest and desire for us to pray. There is nothing about us that is too ordinary, trivial, or troubling for God to help us. We learn in these prayers, expressed in a full range of feelings, that God is willing to take our doubts and angers and is as eager as we to celebrate the good times. By talking with God, we discover within us a creativity that inspires new ideas, new ventures, and new perspectives for looking at old problems. Above all, through prayer, we can live in the knowledge that nothing can separate us from God's love.

These chapters are benchmarks of daily life, finding us giving praise, at home with our families, in times of trouble, learning life lessons, seeking comfort and healing, counting our blessings, and celebrating. The prayers and blessings within each chapter—whether asking, confessing, wondering, seeking, doubting, or thanking—are starting places for continued nourishment of mind and spirit. Sometimes the only prayers we have to offer are our fears and angers; at other times, we are childlike and brief. But always, we are assured of God's attention.

In the light of this truth, reading and pondering these prayers becomes like planting seeds. As you read, it is our hope that you will be reminded of the joy and security that comes from companionship with a God who welcomes our joys and concerns, our laughter and tears.

Praise and Abundance

*O Lord, no matter what life
sends my way, I will praise you in the
morning, sing of you in the noonday sun,
and glorify you in the evening hours.
You alone are worthy of my complete,
unending praise, and may your name
be glorified on earth forevermore.
In Jesus' name, amen.*

Outdoors a storm may rage, the sun may beat down, the snow may fall, but, Lord, you provide me with shelter from these elements.

Whenever I sit by a fireplace, whenever I lie down to sleep, whenever I hear raindrops falling on my rooftop in the morning, may I remember to lift my praise to you, my God. For in your goodness to me, you have granted me the blessings of refuge and safety within the walls of this home.

Thanks-living

Some prayers are best left infinite,
God of all good gifts.
This will be an ongoing conversation between us.
Each day, I discover new gifts you offer me,
and my list of reasons to be thankful grows.
As I gratefully accept your gifts and cherish them,
guide me to become a person who shares with
others so that they, too, can live abundantly.
May someone, somewhere, someday say of me,
"I am thankful to have this person in my life."

PRAISE WELLS UP within my soul, dear God, when I consider the friends you have placed in my life along the way.

We can know the pleasure of conversation, laughter, tears, encouragement, honesty, and love within the context of friendship.

It is true that sometimes we have our differences, but forgiveness and understanding have healed and held our hearts together.

And as we walk arm in arm through whatever lies ahead, good or bad, I will remember to praise you for these friends who make my journey a more joyful experience.

Sing Praise for Today

May you celebrate this day with all your heart.
Rejoice in the beauty of its light and warmth.
Give thanks for the air and grass and sidewalks.
Let gratitude for other faces flow into your soul.
And cherish the chance to work and play,
to think and speak, knowing this —
all simple pleasures are opportunities for praise.

Those who have nurtured me as I have grown up are my family, Lord. We even seem to share the same imperfections. As I learn to appreciate these loved ones, I realize how wonderful it is that there are people to whom I will always belong, how wonderful it is that they look out for my well-being and do their best to love me.

Sometimes my expectations were too high, and I was unfair in my assessment of their efforts. But as I learn to let go of those expectations, I can warm to the memories of their shining moments of kindness, patience, thoughtfulness, and protection. Then my happiness at belonging to them and being loved by them begins to write a song of praise to you in my heart.

Three Squares

I often take for granted the "three squares" (and sometimes more) that I eat each day, God. But next time I pause before a meal to ask your blessing on it, help me to get beyond the ritual, to the true heart of gratitude and praise for your provision.

I have rarely, if ever, known hunger, and you have blessed me with so much that I have enough to share. May my thanks to you come full circle and reach out to bless others.

Praise is due to you,
O God...
You visit the earth and water it,
you greatly enrich it;
the river of God is full of water;
you provide the people with grain,
for so you have prepared it.
You water its furrows abundantly,
settling its ridges,
softening it with showers,
and blessing its growth.
You crown the year with your bounty;
your wagon tracks overflow with richness.
The pastures of the wilderness overflow,
the hills gird themselves with joy,
the meadows clothe themselves with flocks,
the valleys deck themselves with grain,
they shout and sing together for joy.

—Psalm 65:1, 9–13

When I pay my bills this month, help me to consider the ways in which you have provided the means for me to write each check.

Employment, savings, outside financial resources and gifts, health, well-being, skills, abilities, family, friends—some or all of these things have been instrumental in generating my current ability to make ends meet. And whether there is little or much remaining in reserve, God, I thank you for helping me once again to meet my obligations and enjoy what you have provided.

Lord, I truly desire my life to be fruitful and productive, especially in your eyes. Please help me break up any rocky, hard-hearted resistance to you in my life. Amen.

GOD, YOU HAVE GIVEN ME abilities and skills
that enrich my life and the lives of those around
me. I gain pleasure and fulfillment in being able
to use my gifts and talents in this world to make
it a more liveable place. Let the work of my hands
bring praise to you. And may the intentions of my
heart honor you as I use what you have given me
to accomplish the work of spreading goodness
and love.

Small Cog

The work I do helps make the world go 'round,
God. However, it sometimes seems like an awfully
small cog in an awfully big machine. Without my
cog, though, the machine would be in trouble. So
I praise you for my job, for the purpose it serves
in the world's big picture, and for the provision
it brings to my life. Help me to work diligently,
giving my best effort and enjoying the rewards
of my labor, as you strengthen me to do it well.

THE INTENSITY OF LIFE becomes so very overwhelming sometimes, Lord. But you send relief in the form of the things I enjoy doing. They give me a break from the stress-filled parts of life.

When I forget the necessity of these breaks, please remind me that you also mean for me to have fun.

In praise of your gift of fun and relaxation, God, I will take time right now to schedule a break in my day, if for only ten minutes, to stop and do something I enjoy. Amen.

Loving God,
Open my eyes to your wonders:
the magic of birds flying, the power of a
sunrise, the glory of a blooming rose.
I have witnessed your awesome deeds,
and I want you to take my life
and make it whole.
Amen.

Opportunities

Each day as I look about me,
I discover unlimited opportunities.
Every person I meet is an opportunity to uncover a
biography, see through different eyes, find a friend.
Each place to which I go is an opportunity to
try a new route, enjoy the scenery along the way,
explore my surroundings, create an adventure.
Each sunrise, flower, book, meal, walk,
conversation — each encounter in life —
is an opportunity to seize the day.
God, let my life be lived in praise to you as
I take hold of the opportunities you give me.

AND GOD IS ABLE to provide you with every
blessing in abundance, so that by always having
enough of everything, you may share abundantly
in every good work.

—2 Corinthians 9:8

Lord,
I'm glad that the more I give, you give.
Thank you for your abundance.
Amen.

Sharing

We are blessed to live in a country so full of riches, Lord, that we take most of them for granted. Yet we know there are places in the world where children must go to bed hungry, and their mothers cry late into the night because they don't know what tomorrow will bring. Thank you for blessing us with your abundance, Lord. May we have hearts to share what we have with others, and may we never cease to praise you for all you have given to us. Amen.

Creations

Lord, a poem by Joyce Kilmer says,

> *I think that I shall never see*
> *A poem lovely as a tree....*
> *Poems are made by fools like me*
> *But only God can make a tree.*

The praise in my heart for your creation echoes the poet's words. The trees, birds, mountains, streams, and the moon and stars put me in awe of your skill. All the creatures I see, from kittens to kangaroos, from earthworms to elephants, capture my imagination and stir my soul with admiration for your handiwork. My soul cries out, "Magnificent!"

My mouth is filled with your praise,
and with your glory all day long.

—*Psalm 71:8*

Almighty God, I haven't failed to notice that each day begins with a sunrise and ends with a sunset. I know that's your way of wrapping us in your glory. That you—who placed the stars in the sky and caused the tides to ebb and flow—also created me is sometimes more than I can comprehend. You alone are the source of every breath I take. Great and mighty are you, God, and greatly to be praised. Amen.

Thank you, God, for creating ME!
In your womb I have been fashioned;
your Spirit dwells within me;
truly I am wonderfully, marvelously made!
From your love and wisdom have I come
to this place and time.
To me you have given talent and life and blessings.
To me you have given tasks given to no others.
With joy and gratitude
I celebrate my much-honored existence.
From ages past to eternity,
I have been included in your divine plan.
Thank you, God, for creating ME!

Morning

God, you are so great. It is always the right time
to worship you, but morning is best. Praise for
the dawning light that streams in through this
window. Praise for the sound of the birds as they
flit through the air. Praise for the little spider
crawling along the ceiling. Praise for the flowering
plants, even those weeds growing by the house.
Praise for the neighbors walking down the
sidewalk and the clouds moving by in the sky.
Most of all, praise for the breath that keeps flowing
in and out of my lungs. Yes, this is the greatest
thing of praise—that you alone are my life, all life
itself. Without you, all is dust. Praise...for you.

*It is the duty of all nations to
acknowledge the providence of Almighty
God, to obey His will, to be grateful for
His benefits, and humbly implore
His protection and favor.*

—George Washington

For the Beauty of the Earth

For the beauty of the earth,
for the glory of the skies,
for the love which from our birth
over and around us lies:
Lord of all, to you we raise
this our hymn of grateful praise.

For yourself, best gift divine,
to the world so freely giv'n;
for your love beyond all time,
peace on earth and joy in heav'n:
Lord of all, to you we raise
this our hymn of grateful praise.

—*Folliott S. Pierpoint, altered*

But, as it is written,
"No eye has seen, nor ear heard, nor the
human heart conceived, what God has
prepared for those who love him."
—*1 Corinthians 2:9*

LORD, YOU ALWAYS SURPRISE ME with the blessings you give. My life is full of your joy. Just when I need a kind word, a pat on the back, a helpful nudge, you send someone to offer it. You find a million ways to let me know that you love me.

For to all those who have, more will be
given, and they will have an abundance.
—*Matthew 25:29*

Family and Home

Bless all that happens here, O God.
May we find laughter and love
and strength and sanctuary. Bless
all who visit our home, and may we,
like you, offer comfort,
shelter, and welcome.

Peace in Our Home

Let your peace rest upon our home, dear God.
Help us to love one another as you have loved us.
We fail to reach out the way you have gathered us in.
We forget how to give
when only taking fills our minds.
And, most of all, we need your presence to know we are
more than just parents and children.
We are always your beloved sons and daughters.
Let your peace rest upon our home, dear God.

GOD, THE PEOPLE YOU HAVE PLACED in my life—
the people who make up my family—are a blessing
to me in so many ways. We have traveled many
life-miles together through the good and the bad,
but even in our darkest moments, we have known
a bond that is beyond explaining. It is the bond of
family love. Thank you for placing that bond
within our hearts, for by it we are drawn and
held together, whatever may come.

The Faces of Love

Bless my family, Lord. They are a gift from you,
evidence of your unwillingness for me to be alone.
Until I see you face to face, may the faces of those
I love be to me as your own.

I will walk in my house
with blameless heart.
I will set before my eyes no vile thing.
—*Psalm 101:2–3 NIV*

IN OUR FAMILY, LORD, you have made a home in
our hearts for one another. By the lessons you have
helped us learn together, by ways of showing us
how to appreciate the uniqueness each of us brings
to the family unit, by the kindnesses you have
encouraged in our attitudes and actions toward
each other, we have grown close in love and joy.
Let the welcome always remain between us as we
gratefully enjoy all the goodness that you bring to
our relationships.

Tending a Marriage

Marriage, Lord, is like a garden:
You don't keep digging up a plant to see if its roots are
growing! Sustain us, for there are seasons of fading
flowers just as there are seasons of blossom and fruit.
While ripening to become useful, may we love one
another with the same trust and patience you,
gardener of the world, show toward us.

I want to be a help and an encouragement to my family, God, but sometimes my ideas of how to do that are different from theirs.

Please grant me wisdom and discernment to know what will work best for each person in each unique situation.

Help me remember that developing a listening ear is the first step toward having an understanding heart.

And show me how to use humor to help keep things in perspective.

LORD, WE THANK YOU FOR THIS HOME that you have provided for us as a shelter in a storm and a place where we can always find consolation and love. Forgive us for complaining if the roof leaks or the grass needs to be mowed. Make us grateful always, and in all ways, for the wonderful blessing of having a place to call home. We pray that you will dwell in our house so that we might always come home to you. In Jesus' name, amen.

Bless these children, God.
Keep them growing in mind and body.
Keep them ever moving and reaching out
toward the objects of their curiosity.
And may they find, in all their
explorations, the one thing that
holds it all together: your love.

Calming the Storm

Bless us as we weather family conflict.
We all have certain needs to be met,
certain ways of trying to
fulfill our dreams.
Yet each of us seeks this one
basic thing in the midst of it all: love.
Simply love.

LORD, I WANT SO MUCH FOR EVERYONE in my
family to know you, to turn to you, and to walk
with you. But when I bring them to you in prayer,
I hear you telling me that you want me to know
them, to turn toward them, and to walk with them.
I understand, Lord. Please use me today, in any
way you choose, to bring those I love into your
eternal family. In Jesus' precious name, I pray.
Amen.

A Roof Over Our Heads

Bless this roof over our heads, and keep it from leaking. But more than that, move us to give thanks for the next rainstorm. Because you provide more than a good roof—we need to remember that. And our neighbors' crops need watering more than we need to stay dry.

Sanctuary

Source of all life and love, let this family
be a place of warmth on a cold night,
a friendly haven for the lonely stranger, a small
sanctuary of peace in the midst of swirling activity.
Above all, let all its members seek to reflect the
kindness of your own heart, day by day.

Refuge

Enter and bless this family, Lord,
so that its circle will be where quarrels
are resolved and relationships mature;
where failures are forgiven and
new directions are found.

In many different relationships,
dear God, I have found the elements
of what makes me feel at home:
in the conversation of close friends,
in the smiles of helpful neighbors,
in the laughter of family celebrations,
and especially in the peace of your presence.
Wherever you have sprinkled love, joy, peace, patience,
kindness, goodness, faithfulness, and gentleness,
there I have discovered a place for my soul to rest,
a place to call home.

Home, Blessed Home

Home. The word rolls on the tongue like bubble gum, soft and sweet and reminiscent.

Where better to think of you, Lord, than at home?

It is where we have our history, begin our traditions, make our rites of passage.

It is where we are first loved, first safe, first found to be special.

It is where we are sheltered and nourished, then equipped and sent on our way.

Throughout it all, you sit invisibly in our midst, yet are central, blessing our kitchens, where we receive and provide nourishment; bedrooms, giving us restorative sleep; yards and gardens, connecting us with your creation; windows and doors, letting in light and air; basements and attics, sustaining us in ways we often overlook; living rooms, arranging us in "come as you are" circles of families and friends.

We feel your blessing in our lived-in homes.
Help us see the beauty, the opportunities in them.

Bless us — the homebodies.

Telling the Family Tale

Thank you for the gift of family memories. Playing "I Remember" can be such fun, Lord, especially when sharing it with grandchildren. Hopefully, like relay runners, they will be here to pick up their part of our family tale.

LORD GOD, I WANT TO BUILD a strong family by emulating all the good aspects of family life I have experienced or have seen others enjoy. I know that this will require spending time with each other, which means I need you to help me prioritize the relationships with my spouse and children above my other responsibilities.

Nurturing family life will also mean creating and maintaining a safe and healthy environment, where honesty and respect will thrive. Please teach me to be authentic, to value each family member's unique individuality, and to communicate genuine love in my attitudes, words, and actions.

It is good, dear God,
to be a part of this family:
circle of love, place of rest,
bastion of peace.
When every other source of comfort fails,
this is where I return.
Thank you for being in our midst.

Grace for the Family Reunion

We come today, O God, as near strangers gathered from scattered lives, from families who no longer live close by. Be the common thread running through our reuniting as we recall and rededicate our ancestors' memory.

Bless us, Lord, the next generation, as we take our place as the ancestors-to-be. Bless and guide the young ones, our descendants. Help us be worthy of their remembering.

Through this meal and catching up, embrace us and send us back to our distant homes renewed, refreshed, and revitalized until we once again join hands with you around the family table.

GOD, THANK YOU for the special people who over the years have been just like family to me. I love to think of the times we've spent together, of the way they've influenced my life for the better, of their abiding love and care for me. There have been times when they've seemed even more like family to me than anyone else. Please bless these dear members of my extended family, and keep them always in your care.

God,
as the kids go off to school today,
I pray that you will put a circle of angels
around them to protect them and keep them safe.
Help them to learn and to love to learn.
Help them to be kind to other kids,
and let the other kids be kind to them.
I pray that each one of them will be a light for you.
In Jesus' name, amen.

Blessing a Stepfamily

Bless this gathering of what, at first glance, looks like mismatched parts, encircling God, for we want to become a family. Guide us as we step closer to one another, but not so close as to crowd.

Heal wounds from past events that made this union possible. Bless the children with the courage to try new relatives, new traditions, new homes. Empower them in their anger, helping them know that it is okay and that tears are healing. Assure them that they have the strength to live in two worlds and hearts big enough to love others.

Make us, the step-adults, worthy of this love, for it comes at great cost. Help us respect previous traditions and loves and not step too close in our need to belong. For even in the midst of celebrating, there is mourning.

Remind us to take baby steps as we become all you have in mind. Your presence will be our companion, your love our protection, and your wisdom our guidance in this awesome responsibility. Step closer, loving God, and lead us.

When all is quiet, and I cannot hear a voice
or a footstep, a television or a slamming door, I will
thank you, Lord, for this silent revelation of how
the members of my family fill up my days with
activity, making our home vibrant.

It's true that I need these moments of solitude to
re-energize for the relentless challenges of family
life. But I'm deeply grateful to you for each one
who daily brings special personality, strength,
beauty, and perspective into our family.

My prayer for each one of them is that our home
will be a place where they learn to embrace the
wonder and joy of being who you've created
them to be.

In the Blink of an Eye

Just yesterday the children were babies;
overnight, they have jobs, homes,
and babies of their own.
Overnight change, Lord,
is comforting, though reminding me
that nothing stays the same.
Not tough times, not good ones,
just the blending of one stage into another.
I am grateful for the movement
with you at my side.

On Becoming a Grandparent

Thank you for the gift of ancestral faith. May I, as I take my place in the family portrait as the previous generation, continue to keep you, everlasting God, as the centerpiece of our family, for your love is as ageless and steadfast as the wind calling my name.

Watch over the grandchildren as you have over me in your special ways. Listen as I call out their names in echoes of those family prayers shared on my behalf through a lifetime of faith-full love.

God of the ages,
you have been faithful to all
generations. We lift up everyone
in our family to you, those who
barely know you and those who
wait expectantly to see your holy face.
We pray for each cherished soul, Lord, and
ask that you would always keep each
and every one of them in your grace.
If a day ever passes when we fail to
mention each family member's name
in prayer, we pray you will guide and
protect them all just the same.
Amen.

Grace

Bless this food that we eat.
Let it remind us once again that
the soul, like the body, lives and grows by
everything it feeds upon. Keep us drinking
in only the good and the pure,
for your glory. Amen.

Family life is often pedestrian: working, cooking, washing, fixing, building, teaching, learning. It is sometimes painful: being misunderstood, having to give or receive discipline, losing someone, changing, growing.

Yet family life has the power to comfort deeply: feeling accepted, being protected, getting tucked in at night, receiving sympathy. And it offers some of the best moments we will ever experience with others—adventuring, playing, laughing, teasing, hugging, holding. In my family life, God, you have given me a safe place of belonging, where I can experience all the facets of life.

For Our Family

May your eyes look kindly upon this family, Lord,
for we need your love and guidance in our lives.
This is a family that seeks to do the right things—
to work hard for a living,
to raise children who will contribute to society,
and to be a blessing in our neighborhood.
But we know we need your constant help to do
these things.
May we be filled with love and happiness—
all of us who live in this home:
by fulfilling our responsibilities, day in and day out;
by being accountable in all our actions;
by giving whenever we can, even when it hurts;
by nurturing warmth and understanding among us;
and by looking out for the best interests of others.
Please grant our requests according to your great
goodness. Amen.

Neighborly Blessing

Bless my neighbor today.
But keep me from telling him that
I've got his good in mind.
Only let him discover it in my smile,
in my encouraging words,
and in my helping hand.

Real Joy

I'm a mom! A real live, flesh-and-blood mother. I get so overjoyed when I look at the kids — whether they're playing or sleeping or taking a bath. I always wanted children, God, and I am so thankful that it was part of your will. Thank you for your generosity to me, Lord. Thank you, and amen.

I AM GROWN UP and on my own now, Lord.

But tonight my dad will change my oil and check the brakes on my car for me.

Last month, my mom made a birthday dinner for my brother, and we all celebrated together.

My sister and I had breakfast at a little restaurant in town a few weeks ago.

My grandma rode to church with me on Sunday.

My nephews want me to take them mountain biking.

I know there are many people who, like me, do not have a spouse and children yet, God. So I ask you to bless them, as you have blessed me, with an abundance of relationships through family and friends. Fill their lives with the kinship for which they long and for which you have made them.

Bless These Gifts

*Bless, O Lord, these good gifts of food and drink.
Because they have come directly from your hand,
we know they are already blessed in great measure.
But may this recognition of your goodness in
giving add to our joy in partaking.*

My home is not found in the house where I live,
nor in the community or country of my upbringing.
I could travel far and wide and never settle in one
place; I could lose my belongings in a fire or flood;
I could bid farewell to those I love most, and still
my home would not be lost. How can this be?
Because it's true that one's home is where one's
heart is, and to this day my heart remains securely
in your hands, God. You are my truest home,
wherever I might live and whomever I might love
in this life. I can always come home to you.

Bless My Pets

God of beasts and critters,
bless them, for they bless me
even when they shed on the couch
and don't come when called.
They love without strings and
share the simplest joys of walks
and catnaps in the sun,
slowing me to a pace
you recommend.

Bless This Mess

The house is a mess, Lord, and because of it,
my attitude is a matching mood.
Like handwriting on the wall of my
grumpy heart, I got your message:
'Tis far wiser to hunt for first crocuses on spring days
than to look for lost socks in the laundry; to rake
leaves into piles for jumping than to clean piles of
grunge in the corners; to chase giggles rising from a
child's soul like dandelion fluff than to sweep out dust
balls from beneath the beds.
Bless, O Lord, this wonderful mess,
and send me out to play.

First Grace in a New Home

Join us for a meal, Lord, on our makeshift table of boxes and leftovers of our old life as we make a new home. May your love, like the logs we brought from the woodpile back home to lay on a new hearth, be the spark we need to make this move one of growth and success. Be with us in our lonely, homesick moments. Guide us to new neighbors so that our daily bread may once again be the nourishing center for friends. Bless this crackers and cheese meal, Lord; it is the first communion in a new start.

Lord,
heal the differences between me
and my spouse. We argued and then let the sun go
down on our anger. We said things that we can't take
back, and shameful words were spoken. Please give me
the grace to ask for forgiveness and to offer forgiveness.
I ask this in the name of Jesus, amen.

THANK YOU, GOD, for the ability to get away from it all. I pray for traveling mercies and some quality family time on this trip. You know what we each need, so I ask for a bit of joy and respite for each of us. Amen.

Lord,
I feel the need to pray for my neighbors.
I don't see anyone going to church services or hear
them talking about you. I'd like to be your light in
what seems to be darkness, so I'm asking that you
prepare their hearts for anything that I might say.
Help me not to offend, not to be shy,
and not to miss an opportunity.
In Jesus' name I pray, amen.

I'm not feeling very safe in my own home
these days, God. I pray that you would place a hedge
of angels around this dwelling and prevent all evil
from crossing it. Keep us safe, and help us
to accept your protection. Amen.

Perfectly Formed

Lord, God, I thank you for this new baby.
Perfectly formed, perfectly content to be held and
nurtured. Your Word says that you know us before
we are born and knit us in the womb. As I look at
this delicate creation, your power and wisdom
astound me. Thank you for this baby and the
miracle of procreation.

Life Lessons

*Let me do what lies clearly
at hand, this very minute, Lord. Grant
me the insight to see that too much
planning for the future removes me from
the present moment. And this is the only
existence, the only calling I have been
given — to do right now what is necessary.
Nothing more, nothing less. Thus may
I use this next moment wisely.*

I HAVE LEARNED, LORD, that no matter what
happens around me in this world, love is able to
find the best path for my life. When I follow love's
lead, I can never go wrong. Sometimes my selfish
motives try to masquerade as love, but they have
always been discovered for what they are, because
true love is selfless.

Love takes the difficult path if that is what is
required of it, and, to be truthful, I have wished at
times for another way. But love sees the goal and
does not lose hope. It knows when to hold on and
when to let go.

Your love for me, God, has been my perfect
example. Help me to aspire to love as you do,
to follow your example today and always.

Welcome others.
Welcome yourself.
Welcome God.

Finding Joy

The secret to joy, I have discovered, is in finding joy's source. Moods may come and go, but joy can remain through them all when you, God, remain my wellspring of joy. Knowing that you are true to your word, I have confidence in your promises, and this brings a constant flow of rejoicing in my spirit. When circumstances trouble me, help me focus on the assurances you have given in Scripture and let your joy fill me once again.

Happiness resides
not in possessions
and not in gold;
the feeling of happiness
dwells in the soul.

—*Democritus*

Forgiving

Let me know the tranquility
of forgiving today, O Lord.
I have held my peace, doused my anger.
Now it is time to extend my hand.

You have promised that you will keep me in perfect peace when I fix my thoughts on you. I know from experience, Lord, that this principle of peace holds true as I face all kinds of challenges.

When David kept his focus on how great you are, Goliath fell. Likewise, when I remain calm, placing my trust in you, my biggest problems are cut down to size. Thank you for the many times and ways in which you have helped me continue to learn this life lesson. Increase my peace, I pray, Lord, as I trust you.

Prayer for the Right Words

Thank you, God, for the wisdom
to know when to speak,
what to say, and how to say it.
Guard my mouth today from any
form of foolishness,
that in all circumstances
I might honor you with my words.

DEAR GOD, it seems that patience is a lifelong lesson. I can be perfectly patient one day, but when I become stressed out, troubled, or annoyed, my patience becomes a lost virtue. Teach me how to deal with my emotions when I know I should (but don't want to) extend the grace of being patient and understanding with other people. Remind me that I often need that same grace. Grant me empathy for the ones who need it from me today.

A gentle tongue is a tree of life.

—*Proverbs 15:4*

Getting Control

Self-discipline has brought renewed freedoms
to my life, God. Getting control over out-of-control
areas that have enslaved me has kept me from going
to destructive extremes. You are teaching me that to
have a healthy handle on my greatest weakness is to
bring a new level of enjoyment to all of life.

So I ask you to grant me the strength to gain and
maintain self-control in the area in which I am
most vulnerable to the tyranny of excess. Allow
these lessons of self-discipline I'm learning to keep
me free today.

Lord,
it's hard for me to come to you when
I've made such a mess of things. But I know
that you are the only place I can turn. Examine my
heart, Lord, and you will see how sorry I am for the
mistakes I've made. I ask for your forgiveness first of
all. I also ask that you would give me your insight
into how I can make the best of this situation.
Rescue me through your mercy, Lord.
Amen.

I BELIEVE THAT HOW I LIVE affects those
around me, Lord God. I do not speak and act in a
vacuum. Whether I like it or not, my example will
be followed by someone. For this reason, I believe
that my efforts to develop goodness in my life are
of vital importance as others look on. Help me,
please, to embrace good habits, good attitudes, and
good principles by which to live, so that anyone
who might choose to follow in my footsteps will
enjoy the benefits of a life well lived.

Call to Action

We know, Lord, that action is the proper fruit of knowledge and all spiritual insight. But so often we wish only to think and muse, without ever doing good toward anyone. Yes, it's easier to know the good than to do it. It's more comfortable to be right than to do the right thing. It's more convenient to sit on the sidelines and give advice than it is to enter the game.

Change us, God! Open our eyes so that we may see the needs around us. Show us the poor — and all the ways we can help. Help us to take the more difficult route of service. Help us to make friends and bond with those who are different. Help us to take all we know and put it into every resource at hand, so that action may result for the good of all.

*Security, loving God, is going to sleep
in the assurance that you know our hearts before
we speak and that you are waiting, as soon as you
hear from us, to transform our concerns into hope
and action, our loneliness into companionship,
and our despair into dance.*

LORD GOD, YOU ARE FAITHFUL and committed to what you promise. In a world where contracts aren't worth the paper on which they are printed, it's my desire to stand out as one whose word is as good as gold.

Help me learn the kind of faithfulness you demonstrate. I need to follow through on what I promise, even if it hurts me to do so. Help me to be trustworthy—to keep confidences, to be a truth-teller, and to do what is honest at all times. Help me to stick to my commitments, making them a priority in my life.

Thank you for your perfect example, God, from which I can draw inspiration and guidance.

I learn gentleness from you, God, in the breezes that touch my face, in the way of a mother with her young, in the gradual changing of the seasons. Gentleness in life is seen in grace, tact, empathy, tenderheartedness. Thank you for being so gentle with my heart. And now that your gentleness has shown me how to behave, help me to emulate you by gently and carefully touching the lives of those around me.

Lord,
the more I learn about you, the more I love you.
And the more I love you, the more I want to change
the world for you. I want to create mountains of faith
for all to see, but I hear you telling me that I need to
be content to build those mountains one small pebble
at a time. Please keep me faithful in the little things,
Lord, that you might be greatly praised.
In Jesus' name, amen.

Lord,
sometimes I'm so busy looking
for your will in my life that I forget
to look for ways I can fit my life into your will.
It's your agenda that I want for my life, Lord, not my
own. Please lead me to those discoveries, those people,
those Bible verses that will show me the direction you
want me to take. For I surely know that unless
I'm going with you, I'm going the wrong way.
In Jesus' name, amen.

"THE MILK OF KINDNESS" nurtures our love for one another, God. I have learned that the soft answer truly does disarm anger, that the unexpected act of mercy can transform even an enemy into a friend. Today, I ask for opportunities to put this principle into practice. May my random yet purposeful acts of kindness be small blessings that reproduce in the actions of others, making this world a more pleasant place to live.

Insights

In the course of my lifetime, you have granted
me many moments of special insight—those
"aha!" experiences. In these moments, the eyes
of my understanding have been suddenly opened
to truth, and I have seen more clearly the way
I ought to live. But these insights are only made
complete when I implement them in everyday
situations, Lord, and I often struggle to do that.
So I ask you to bring these lessons home to me,
by integrating them into how I live. Transform
my mere insight into the grace of insightful living,
I pray.

*The appetite of the lazy
craves, and gets nothing,
while the appetite of the
diligent is richly supplied.*

—*Proverbs 13:4*

YOUR PLAN FOR US, Lord, is that we follow
those who follow the right and the good. Your
spirit fills those who walk in humility, patience,
and self-sacrifice. Please open our eyes that we
may see those gentle faces beckoning us upward
and onward in a spirit of love. They are all
around us, we're certain. Only open our eyes!

A Blessing for Failure

*Bless my attempts at success, Lord, though
I know many of them will end in failure.
I pray that you will even bless my failures,
for I also know that never risking
is a sure sign of sloth and a questioning
of your constant goodwill toward me.*

Seeing Around Corners

I'm getting a crick in my neck trying to see
around the bend, God. I'm wearing myself
out second-guessing. Teach me to live in today,
needing just a small glimpse down the road.
No need to borrow worry.

Do not worry about anything,
but in everything, by prayer and supplication
with thanksgiving, let your requests be made known
to God. And the peace of God, which surpasses all
understanding, will guard your hearts and
your minds in Christ Jesus.

—*Philippians 4:6–7*

A Sign

To those scanning a night sky, you sent a star.
To those tending sheep on a silent hill, you sent
a voice. What sign, Lord, are you sending me—
so I can be and do all you intend? Let me
hear, see, and accept it when you do.

Answers

We pray but don't feel answered, Lord.
Help us understand that, regardless of the
answers we want, being connected to you through
prayer is changing us into "can do" people.
We can find solutions,
we can try again.
Looking back, we understand
you did answer.

Listening for God

Lord, we've tossed our prayers aloft, and hopefully, expectantly, we wait for your answers. As we do, we will listen, for you speak in the voice of nature. We will see you as a companion in the face and hand of a friend; feel you as a sweet-smelling rain, a river breeze; believe you can provide encouragement, direction, and guidance for those who have only to ask. We feel your presence.

I came before you in my need,
begging, pleading,
my desires to fulfill.

"Turn brass into gold
and stones into bread,"
I implored.

Through planet turns
and season changes
most earnestly did I entreat,
confident of my prayers' answers.

With absence of thunderbolt
or angelic announcement,
the miracle was done.
Now am I satisfied.

Though no surplus of bread
nor gold have I,
yet transformation is realized.

The God of surprises
fulfills me beyond my asking.
The miracle is within —
It is I who am changed.

Empty Rooms

Finally, my children all have homes of their own. This house feels so much bigger. I know it can become a cold and lonely space or a warm, comforting haven. You will make the difference, Lord. Pack these rooms with all the good memories until the next time my children visit, bringing their children, too, along with them.

In a New Place

May God grant that you
will find happiness in your new destination.
In the transition from country to city: peace.
In the move from friends to strangers: acceptance.
In the letting go of the old
to embrace the new: confidence.
In the challenge of new work: unflagging zeal.
In all these ways, may the blessing
of God be upon you.

Being Within Being

Blessed is the one who can look upward and recognize divine glory in the sun and clouds, who can look downward and be moved to praise by stones and flowers.

Blessed is the one who can look inside and find being within being, knowing one is never alone, certain there is more to be known than to be seen.

Over mountains
and over valleys
and over oceans
and over rivers
and over deserts,
one says: Blessed are you, Lord,
our God, king of the world,
who makes the works of creation. . . .
Over rain
and over good news,
one says: Blessed are you, Lord, our God,
ruler of the world,
who is God and who does good things.

Lessons From the School of Life

So far, I have learned:
Silence speaks volumes when words dry up,
and solitude never needs fearing.
Giving is clearly the best joy of all,
and thankfulness is the goal of all living.
Wisdom will enter with force unannounced,
and grace goes wherever God is willing.
Relinquishing all—this is life's success.
And seeking your purpose, the meaning.
Thank you, Master Teacher!

Imperfect

Only machines run perfectly—for awhile—and we know exactly what to expect from them. But we are different, Lord. We often do the unexpected, certainly the imperfect.

Give us the joy of diversity, the pleasure of indulging variety in our approaches to life. Being incomplete, we reach our hands to you, expecting help. And that is good, since only in you can we be perfectly fulfilled.

Holy God, you have shown me light and life.
You are stronger than any natural power.
Accept the words from my heart
that struggle to reach you.
Accept the silent thoughts and feelings
that are offered to you.
Clear my mind of the clutter of useless facts.
Bend down to me, and lift me in your arms.
Make me holy as you are holy.
Give me a voice to sing of your love to others.

—Ancient Christian prayer, written on papyrus

Darkest Before the Dawn

Teach us to know, God, that it is exactly at the point of our deepest despair that you are the closest. For at those times, we can finally admit we have wandered in the dark, without a clue. Yet you have been there with us all along. Thank you for your abiding presence.

Of Love and Vulnerability

May you avoid the temptation to treat love
as a mere commodity today. It is a most precious
gift, bound up within the soul of another. It can
only be given and received at the price of great
vulnerability. Blessings upon all who know it,
really know it.

When I was a boy in my father's house,
still tender, and an only child of my mother,
he taught me and said,
"Lay hold of my words with all your heart;
keep my commands and you will live.
Get wisdom, get understanding;
do not forget my words or swerve from them.
Do not forsake wisdom, and she will protect you;
love her, and she will watch over you."
—Proverbs 4:3–6 NIV

The Cure for Anger

O God, you see that when anger blinds the eyes
the truth disappears.
Give patience for rage, warmth in place of wrath.
And wrap all in the humility
that comes from knowing:
They are all innocent in their own way.

How Am I Doing?

All cats appear gray in the dark, Lord, and I
have no clear sense of how well I'm doing. I
need feedback. Help me sort it into piles of
what to keep, what to discard.

Remind me to offer feedback, for others look to
me for their validation; a simple "You're doing
great" goes a long way. I'm listening for your
feedback, longing to hear, "Well done, good
and faithful servant."

Help Is at Hand

Sometimes, Lord, the simplest ideas are wisest.
When we wonder how to pray, the answer is
readily "at hand":

Thumb reminds us to pray for those closest:
family, friend, neighbor;

Index for our guides, teachers, preachers;

Middle for leaders and those in authority;

Ring, the weakest finger, reminds us to pray
for the helpless, sick, and poor;

Pinkie for ourselves.

And so, O God, we come holding out our hands,
knowing yours is outstretched and waiting.

Acceptance

*Lord, help me to learn to accept the things
in life that seem unfair, to see beyond
present frustrations or stubbornness
and learn from the situations you
have presented to me.*

I PRAY, LORD, that I will be as quick to see my
own faults as I am to recognize the faults of others.
I just keep judging people, although your word
calls that sin. I am not perfect, and I always pray
that you will be understanding of my humanness.
What I need to understand is that we are all
human, all fallible. If I lapse, quickly remind me of
that. May we commit together to helping me
overcome this terrible habit? I will try, but I plead
for your help along the way. Amen.

COME, GOD OF WANDERERS and pilgrims, be
our companion and guide. Let prayer be a bridge,
a meeting place spanning icy floodwaters.

We sense you near and are grateful to no longer
be alone, knowing that choosing to live and relying
on you as our guide is a move as major as paddling
onto the deepest, wildest river.

There's an easy way and a hard way to do river
rapids. To do life. With you, O God, as guide,
we joyfully move into the swift currents of life.

Lord,
help me to be a happier person.
If I am to be a witness for you, I have to change
the way I look at the world — and the way the world
perceives me. I'm sorry that I am such a slow learner,
but with your help, I CAN do this.
Here's to true joy, Lord!
Amen.

Lord,
today a homeless person asked me
for a handout. I gave him a bus token and directions
to the nearest shelter. Now I want to pray for his soul
and his spirit. His eyes and his posture spoke volumes;
please lift him up. Help him to see his way clear to
find a job and a home. I pray for the volunteers who
will meet him; help them to be patient and to see the
man behind the clothing. With your help, he can rise
above his present circumstances. With your love, he
can become whole again. He is someone's child,
perhaps someone's brother. But he is also your
child, and I pray that you will show
concern for him even now.
In Jesus' name, amen.

Your Will

*We can't always know your will, and I know
I often confuse it with my own. But today I am on
my knees begging you to show me your perfect will
in this situation. Help me not to be selfish, not to
manipulate circumstances, and to wait upon you
and your wisdom. Amen.*

Lord, may we take a moment and concentrate on forgiveness. Grant me a forgiving spirit, one that fits with your expectations and commandments. Help me to give up hidden resentments, foolish ill-will, and time-wasting thoughts of other souls along their own paths. Forgiveness does not come naturally to me. But I pray that you will abide with me awhile, so that when I get off my knees, the weight of my unforgiving spirit will lift from my shoulders. Lord, I want to be able to stand before you, forgiven of my own sins, and so I must do the same on earth. Bear with me, stay with me, give me grace. Amen.

Limitless Possibilities

When I was a child, I wanted to be a firefighter. Or maybe a news anchor. That all seemed so exciting. Now that I'm in school and getting a degree, I feel like the whole world is open to me. I can do or be anything. However, I really want to do what you would have me do. Please give me good counsel, help me to be sensitive to your direction, and open and close the doors that will focus me according to your will. Thank you for being with me every moment of the day.

Letting Go

Sometimes, God, I wish I could
control the events in my life that cause me anxiety.
Please help me to let go of my need to control things
and to allow your plan for my life to
unfold before me. I will trust in you,
God, to show me the way.

Lord, I tried to make a difference today,
but it didn't seem to happen.
Either an oak will grow from the acorn
I planted, or I must start over.
Give me the wisdom to know which way
to carry on. In Jesus' name, amen.

Trust in God

God, sometimes, when life takes a confusing turn, I don't understand what your plan for my life must be. But I have learned that when I trust in you, things work out for the best. I give myself to you, God, knowing that you will look after me and those whom I love. When bad things happen, I will search for the lessons you are teaching me. For your watchful eye, your unconditional love, your supportive hands, I am forever grateful.

You have given me more than I ever even hoped or imagined, Lord. I have a nice house and a family that loves me. Here I am, with so much more.

Help me to share what you've given me, to be alert to others in need, and to have a willing heart when you call on me to do something I wouldn't think of on my own.

Open my heart to feel when someone may need my help through a difficult time. Open my eyes so that I can be aware of more than my everyday circle of friends and activities.

Your abundance is overwhelming. Thank you for allowing me to partake of it.

My faith looks up to thee
Thou Lamb of Calvary,
Savior Divine
Now hear me while I pray;
Take all my guilt away
O let me from this day
be wholly Thine.

—Ray Palmer, 1830

Dear Lord and Father of humankind,
Forgive our foolish ways;
Reclothe us in our rightful mind,
In purer lives Thy service find,
In deeper reverence, praise.
— The Brewing of Soma, *by John Whittier*

Today I learned the meaning of the word "humility." It was a hard lesson, but one I needed.

Help me to recover from my embarrassment, to be able to look others in the eyes, and to remember to be kind to others in the same situation. Getting up tomorrow and facing people will be hard, but if you are with me, I will get through it.

Thank you for your tender mercies, God. And now I would ask that you would help me to fall asleep and not dwell on what I cannot undo. Amen.

Lord,
I spend so much time praying
for myself that I often forget to pray
for the rest of the world. I'd like to
spend some time now praying for my family…
my friends and neighbors…pastors…
those on mission fields…
those who will hear your word this week…
schoolteachers…our government and
those in power throughout the world…
the homeless…the sick…those who mourn…
the hungry…the hopeless…and the unsaved.
Amen.

Opting for Hope

Given a choice between hope and despair when trouble hits, Lord, I pick hope. It doesn't trivialize suffering or dismiss evil; it simply trusts your promise to make all things new.

In Times of Trouble

*Lord,
you are so good to give me
just enough light to see my next step,
and you promise that you will never let
the light go out. But sometimes it's scary
to take just one step at a time when I don't
know where I'm going. This is one of those
times, Lord. I want to step out in faith
with you, but I'm afraid. Please fill me
with your courage, your wisdom,
and your perfect sense of direction.
In Jesus' name, amen.*

HELP US, LORD! Everything seems to be spinning out of control, and there's no help in sight but you. Gratefully, we know that putting our trust in you is the most productive thing we can do. For when we aren't in control anymore, you still are. We place all that's happening right now in your hands and ask that you help us sort out solutions to these problems we face. For we know that with you all things are possible.

Prayer for Peace in the Family

Contention and friction in family relationships leave me feeling uneasy, Lord. I long for reconciliation and peace, but I don't know how to make it happen. Help me to do my part in this matter, whether it means speaking the truth in love to someone, letting go of something, seeking or offering forgiveness, praying, or quietly setting an example. Show me how to walk in your way of peace, God, and let that peace permeate each relationship in my life.

Cups Running Over With Anger

God of peace, what are we to do with our anger?
In the wake of trouble, it fills us to overflowing.
Sometimes our anger is the only prayer we can
bring you. We are relieved and grateful to know
that you are sturdy enough to bear all we feel
and say.

Where do we go from here? Is there life after fury?
What will we be without our anger when it's all
that has fueled us?

When we are still, we hear your answer:
"Emptied." But then we would be nothing.
Remind us that, in your redeeming hands,
"nothing" can become of great use, as a gourd
hollowed out becomes a cup or a bowl only when
emptied.

When the time comes for us to empty ourselves of
this abundance of anger, make us into something
useful.

When disaster comes, reminding me of how little control I really have over some things in life, God, I am humbled and made aware again of how much I need you to be my source of strength and comfort.

And when I mourn the loss of temporal possessions, suddenly lost due to unforeseen circumstances, I give thanks that you are the eternal one who will never leave me nor forsake me. In this assurance, I find an indestructible hope and the courage I need to go on.

Lord,
when we have nothing left to hold on to,
you provide us with hope as an anchor for our souls.
We need that hope now, and we pray that you will fill
every broken place in our hearts with its reassuring
light. Thank you, Lord, for in you we have an
unending supply of hope in the midst of uncertainty
and failure. We know that if we could see this
situation through your eyes, we would see how
you will bring us through it.
We place our hope in you and you only.
Amen.

My Mother Died

I don't belong to anyone now, Lord—
my mother died today.
Who will recall the stories of my birth?
My first loose tooth? First day of school?
Who will tell me I'm special, perfect,
and always welcome no matter what?
Reach out to me, a little child again,
lost and frightened and suddenly orphaned.
Stay with me until I fall asleep, and be here
should I awake, frightened. Let me be a child tonight.
Tomorrow I'll be strong, as befitting
the new matriarch of this family.
But for now, Lord, find me, hold me.

I HAVE LOST ONE I LOVE, Lord, and the profound emptiness I feel is unbearable at times. In those moments, I know you are with me, but it may be a while before I can sense your comfort and care. Meanwhile, please keep me safe as I grieve—as I question, as I rage, as I weep, as I sit in silence—waiting to heal and feel whole and alive again.

The word "depression," God, makes me think of a deep hole in the ground. And that's how I feel— like I've fallen into a pit from which I cannot climb out. I can hear life going on above me, but I cannot join in because I cannot get to where everyone else seems to be. Even my desire to try is gone, yet I don't want to stay here. Please grant me the desire and the ability—your grace—to rise up and embrace the gift of life you've given me. Encourage my heart today as I wait for you to lead me into joy.

Prayer for Healing

My health is not what I wish it to be, dear God. And it's hard to enjoy life fully right now.
I long to be free from these physical symptoms, but I don't seem to be getting better. Help me, please.
I ask that you would bring your healing where my strength fails and my ability falls short.

The Lord is good,
a stronghold in a day of trouble;
he protects those who
take refuge in him ...

—*Nahum 1:7*

THE UNKNOWN FRIGHTENS ME sometimes, God, and right now life is so uncertain. How can I know what to do when I don't know what will happen next? How do I know what you intend by this when you seem so silent?

I know this is one of those faith-stretching experiences, but I don't feel up to the challenge right now. Bring your calm to my anxious thoughts; bring your peace to the turmoil in my emotions. You are far bigger than any challenge I will ever face in life. Let this reality be a starting point for my growing trust in your goodness.

The Barriers Inside

Lord, I wish to live a long life,
but I fear growing old.
I want to accomplish great things,
but I fear risking what I already have.
I desire to love with all my heart,
but the prospect of self-revelation
makes me shrink back.
Perhaps for just this day,
you would help me reach out?
Let me bypass these dreads and see instead
your hand reaching back to mine—
right now—just as it always has.
Seeking courage, Lord,
I bundle my fears
and place them in your hands.
Those shadowy terrors that were once
too heavy for me, too weighty even to ponder,
have shrunk in my mind
and—how wonderful!—
withered to nothing in your grasp.

IT'S RARELY EASY to make a life transition. But, God, this one seems especially difficult. I'm trying to be brave, but there is so much uncertainty, and I lack confidence in my ability to successfully adjust to my new situation.

Please walk me through this change, step by step. Help me to not cling stubbornly to the past nor to try looking too far into the future. Where my self-confidence ends, let my confidence in you begin.

The sting of rejection lingers, Lord, as I try to focus on other aspects of life. My hopes for this relationship were different than the reality I face. And even still, I hope for a miracle to come and change how things are. But you know what has happened, and you understand, for you have experienced rejection as well.

You offer me your comfort and friendship, even as I struggle with losing a relationship with one I cared for deeply. Help me to see your love for me, not as a consolation prize, but for what it really is: the truest form of love, the fulfillment of my heart's ultimate longing.

LORD, MY FINANCIAL SITUATION is a major source of stress in my life now, and I'm struggling to believe things will be okay. You've provided for my needs in the past, but I can't see a way out this time. The pressure is mounting, time is running out, and I am crumbling under the weight of it all. That's why I'm sending up this cry for help to you. I know you see my trouble and that you hear my prayer. Please grant me the wisdom, faith, and opportunity I need to discover your provision.

It's such a helpless feeling to watch the ones I love struggle. God, I want to rush in and help them, but I am powerless to do so. I feel frustrated, and I can't help wondering why you don't intervene. But I must trust your wisdom at this time and believe that even while you see all that is happening, you are not indifferent. Your plan is always to build and strengthen us, and you will not give us more than we can bear when we trust in you. So that is where I choose to place my trust right now — in you.

Have mercy on me,
O God, have mercy on me,
for in you my soul takes refuge.
I will take refuge in the shadow of
your wings until the disaster has passed.
I cry out to God Most High, to God,
who fulfills his purpose for me.
He sends from heaven and saves me,
rebuking those who hotly pursue me:
God sends his love and his faithfulness.

—*Psalm 57:1–3 NIV*

Sticks and Stones

No matter how hard I try, someone finds fault with me. I am mortified about the latest criticism. I can't decide whether to run away in shame or storm back and defend my actions. Give me the courage to confront this, Lord.

Keep me calm and open to your soothing power. Help me to remember how I'm feeling now the next time I find fault with someone.

For Everyone in Times of Trouble

O Lord, hear my prayer for all those who are
in trouble this day.

Comfort those who are facing the loss of a loved
one. Be with them as they say good-bye. After the
wrenching grief, let their lonely hours be filled
with fond memories of days gone by. Let them cry
on your shoulder.

Calm those who are passing their days without
work. During this time of financial stress, give
them energy to search for a fulfilling and
worthwhile new job. Assure them that you will
provide; give them your peace.

Heal those who are suffering pain and illness. Let
them find rest and calm as they seek to make the
idle moments pass more quickly. Cradle their
racked minds in your love, and soothe every
irrational thought that seeks to run out of control.

Encourage those who are finding it difficult to believe in the future. Let your hope fill their hearts as they recall all your past faithfulness. Assure them when they doubt the truth of your existence or the validity of your promises. Bring into their lives wise friends who have long known the reality of your love. Let them be assured that you can take care of every need, no matter how large or small.

Uphold those who are being tempted in any way today, especially those who may want to end their lives. Show them that while there is life there is hope, that change is the only constant, and that change for the better is very likely. May they find joy in just one moment at a time. And may that be enough for now.

In all these ways, I ask your blessing upon those in trouble. And please include me, too!

Blessing for This Night

The day has been long, Lord.
Bless me now with stillness and sleep.
I sigh and turn over, knowing that night
will usher in the day with new joys
and possibilities, gifts from your
ever-wakeful spirit.

WHEN LIFE GOES AWRY, Lord, and I need someone to blame, I point a finger at you. Heaven help me, I want it both ways: you as the sender and the fixer of trouble. Help me know you don't will trouble, for what could you possibly gain? And when the good you want for me isn't possible in the randomness of life, remind me that you are with me.

What to Do?

Someone I care about is suffering, Lord, and I feel
helpless. Assure me that a little means a lot and
that I'm sharing your healing love in my notes and
visits. If you need me to do more, send me. I am
like dandelion fluff—small but mighty in
possibility.

A Lesson in Suffering

May I be blessed in this suffering.
May I know that you can use this thing to show me
a mistaken attitude, a destructive behavior.
In that way, may I be blessed
in this suffering,
O Lord, my God.

When trouble strikes, O God, we are restored by small signs of hope found in ordinary places. We receive random acts of kindness from friends, and sometimes even strangers, who share our pain and offer us support. Help us collect these acts as if they were mustard seeds that can grow into a spreading harvest of well-being.

The Gift of Optimism

Enliven my imagination,
God of new life, so that I can see through
today's troubles to coming newness.
Surround me with your caring
so that I can live as if the
new has already begun.

Lord, give me the faith to take the next step, even when I don't know what lies ahead. Give me the assurance that even if I stumble and fall, you'll pick me up and put me back on the path. And give me the confidence that, even if I lose faith, you will never lose me. Amen.

When you pass through the waters,
I will be with you;
and through the rivers,
they shall not overwhelm you;
when you walk through fire
you shall not be burned,
and the flame shall not consume you.

—*Isaiah 43:2*

MY HEART IS HEAVY, God. I realize now, at the
end of the day, that I haven't thought of you once.
I haven't considered how you would want me to
act, whether you had something for me to do, or
if anything I did was simply against your Word.

It's so silly. I know I can't do this on my own, yet
today I took the whole world on as though I'm
the only person who counts. Please forgive me.

Help me not to slide so far into my own plans that
I forget that your timetable is far more important
than anything I could come up with. Again, forgive
me, and let me be always mindful of your presence
in my life. Amen.

Incline your ear to me; rescue me speedily.
Be a rock of refuge for me, a strong
fortress to save me.

—Psalm 31:2

Hopeful Night

In the midst of mourning life's
troubles, you come to us.
In the darkness, your spirit moves,
spreading light like a shower of stars
against a stormy night sky.

LORD, WE KNOW that if life were smooth sailing there would be no need for faith. We thank you for the opportunity to trust you tenaciously, in spite of the obstacles in our paths. Amen.

Out in the Fields

The little cares that fretted me,
I lost them yesterday,
among the fields above the sea,
among the winds at play . . .
among the hushing of the corn,
where drowsy poppies nod,
where ill thoughts die and good are born—
out in the fields of God.

—*Anonymous*

Remind me that you are always with me.
Fill me with your peace,
grant me your mercy,
and lead me in your ways.

PRIDE GOT THE BETTER OF ME TODAY, Lord. You helped me to prepare, you granted me peace, you gave me courage. And I took all the credit. So, here I am, asking even more from you: Please forgive me so that I can get up off my knees as a forgiven person. I ask it in your holy name. Amen.

I need comforting today, God. When I see my friends rocking their babies, it inspires me to think of you doing that for me.

Just to be held by one who loves me more than I can know would give me such a sense of well-being and consolation. Please send someone into my life who can do that for me today. Someone who can be your arms and your presence in my life for just a minute, transforming my distress into manageable moments.

Thank you for being here with me even now. Thank you.

Lord,
I am facing a difficult situation today.
Please be present with me and help me
to hear your voice above all the rest.
Give me strength and wisdom and a
double dose of your wondrous love.
Thank you and amen.

Today is one of those days, Lord, when I have to get on my knees before I can get on my feet. I'm tired, I'm busy, and I can't imagine that I will get through this day. Help me to choose wisely, to think clearly, and to do all that must be done. I may not have time to pray throughout the day—at least not much more than a brief telegram—but I ask you to be with me and uphold me as only you can. In Jesus' name, amen.

IT OFTEN SEEMS UNFAIR that I am unable to buy nice things for myself or my family, Lord. Help me to see my financial situation as a hidden blessing, teaching me what's really important. The love of my family, the health of my children, the future of my community . . . all these things require my attention.

Help me to let go of frustration and anxiety about money and calmly accept the hard financial knocks that may come my way, knowing that under your watchful care things will work out for the best. Freedom from this worry will let me release my energy to attend to those intangible things that make life rich, full, and joyous.

I'VE HAD THE RUG PULLED OUT from under my feet, Lord. As I pray, fill me with your grace. Help me to accept this new challenge with calm, forgiveness, understanding, and trust in your purpose for my life.

Jesus,
you understand what it means
to bear another's pain. As I sit in
this emergency room, waiting for news of
my loved one, I want to take away the pain in that
room. I want to make it my own. I pray that you will
be with the doctors and nurses and technicians, giving
them wisdom and directing their hands. Please ease
the suffering . . . and calm the fear.
Amen.

Walk by My Side, God

Lord, my steps falter
when I am faced with hard times.
Sometimes it is easy to forget that
your footprints follow next to me in silent
support, no matter how hazardous a path
I must tread. Thank you, God, for that
support. Teach me again and again to
trust in you with each challenge I face.
Be my constant companion as
I walk the path you set
before me, in love.

Healing and Comfort

*You send comfort to me, Lord,
in the breath of the wind that
touches my face, in the warmth
of the sun breaking through the clouds,
in the voices of the crickets and bullfrogs
that sing me to sleep at night.*

*In simple reminders,
you assure me of your presence.*

I HAVE BETTER DAYS and worse days, God.
You know them all. In my better days, you
help me see that life can be good again. In my
worse days, you show me that even when life
is not good, you're the friend who always will
listen, always will encourage, always will
comfort, always will love. Your love never fails.
And that makes all the difference in the world,
especially when I'm feeling unlovely and
unlovable. Thank you, God, for loving me,
whatever the day may bring.

Lord,
I lift up those who are ill and pray for
your healing hand upon them. It's so hard to
understand why many are blessed with good health
while others have to suffer through lingering illness
and pain. But it comforts us to know that in your
mighty power you can make the sick well again. If it
be your will, Lord, please bless those for whom I pray
with your all-powerful, healing touch.
In Jesus' name, amen.

Suffering is never pleasant, Lord,
but you often bring about good in my life
as you help me through the hard times.

I have seen that through adversity
has come increased strength.
Through challenge has come new growth.
Through pain has come greater depth.
Through questioning has come more understanding.
Through grief has come truer empathy.
Through loss has come an ability to cherish.
And through rejection, an incredible
capacity to love has filled my heart.

As I reflect on all I have endured,
I see that from out of the ashes
of suffering, God, you have created
new beauty in my life.

Grant Me Rest

God, I can't help but wonder why you allow pain
in my life. I try to think of all the reasons, but, in
the end, I am still left with questions. I guess that's
where faith comes in. But I don't want my faith in
you to be just a blind belief in something I'm not
sure of. No, I want to find rest in a deep trust in
your ultimate goodness and care for me. Despite
the circumstances, despite the pain, with your
help, God, I will trust that you are holding me
close today.

SOMETIMES HEALING COMES at once as an
instantaneous miracle. But more often, healing
happens in slow motion as a gradual process.
Miracles of healing thrill us but are soon forgotten.
Processes of healing teach us and stay with us
forever. God, let the healing you have brought to
my life be a blessing of growth and insight that
lasts a lifetime and also helps others along the way.

Carry Me

Lord God, today was almost more than I could bear. I am afraid to face tomorrow. How can I know that things will be okay when everything seems so wrong right now? I have no strength left inside to take the next step, so I'm asking you to pick me up and carry me. I know you offer your grace as a gift of sufficiency, providing me with everything I need to go on. I accept your grace right now. Help me rest in the knowledge that you will be with me, taking me through each moment that lies ahead.

People say that time can heal every heart-wound I suffer, Lord. But time seems to stand still, and my wounds go deep. I think of that phrase in Psalm 23: "he restores my soul." But I wonder, can you mend my brokenness? I believe, in time, that you can, but I need you to walk with me through today's heartache. Here is my hand, Lord. Lead my soul to the place of healing and restoration.

Lord,
thank you for the life of the one
we mourn today. We know that it is only
when we turn to you in our grief that we can
experience any relief at all. For in the midst of our
pain, you give us a deep abiding peace . . . a peace that
passes understanding . . . a peace that carries us from
this moment into your future. Thank you, Lord, for
blessing us with your peace — the only thing that will
sustain us through this time of loss and grief.
In Jesus' name, amen.

Every life you have created, Lord, is a gift to be treasured. When that life is lost to us, it is a loss to be mourned. But you assure us that those we love will be a part of our hearts forever, and that we will be reunited with them in your heavenly kingdom. Thank you, Lord, for the good news that lifts us out of the despair we feel. We praise you for your abiding promises and enduring love.

As children, some of us prayed,

> *Now I lay me down to sleep,*
> *I pray the Lord my soul to keep.*
> *Peace and safety till I wake,*
> *This I pray for Jesus' sake. Amen.*

The simplicity of our prayers reflected a simple trust.

Sometimes, Lord, it's good for us to return to simplicity when life gets complicated, to remember the basic things we once knew without question. Bring rest to our bodies and minds through a simple trust in your ability to keep us and care for us. Amen.

As a mother comforts her child,
so I will comfort you...

—*Isaiah 66:13*

IT SEEMS UNCANNY, God, the many times people have been in just the right place, at just the right time, with just the right word or touch as I've struggled through this experience. I can't help but believe that somehow you've had a hand in all those chance encounters. It makes me feel special that you would bother to arrange such specific and meaningful moments of care for me, and I just want to let you know that I'm grateful.

Let Me Be a Healer

I wish to extend my love, Lord.
So give me hands quick to work on behalf of the weak.
Cause my feet to move swiftly in aid of the needy.
Let my mouth speak words
of encouragement and new life.
And give my heart an ever-deepening
joy through it all.

Lighting My Way

I feel healing rising up like the morning sun,
breaking and broadening slowly on the horizon of
my heart. It comes after a long darkness, God, but
I realize now that even in the nighttime of my pain,
you were with me, sending your comfort and care
like the moon and the stars, keeping watch over
my life. Thank you for lighting my way through
the night and bringing the blessing of dawn again.

Man of Sorrows, see my grieving heart this day.
Keep me from feelings of shame, though,
as I let the loss wash over me.
For this is a part of my life, too,
the life only you could give me:
to learn what it means to let go.

Complaints sometimes come first, God, before I can feel free to love you. Sometimes you seem distant and unreasonable, even uncaring. Help me understand why life can be so hurtful and hard. Hear my complaints, and, in the spirit of compassion, show me how to move through pain to rebirth.

Doves on the Horizon

Troubles, dear Lord, have cast us loose from assumptions and certainties, and we are bobbing like rudderless boats on a stormy surf. When all hope seems gone, we spot doves on the horizon.

Doves, like those you sent to Noah and his family to assure them the storm was nearly over. Doves in the phone calls from friends; in the smile of a neighbor; in the wisdom of a caregiver and counselor; in good laughs or hearty, cleansing tears; in the flash of a new idea, a goal, a dream.

We can recognize landmarks now and see our way through the storm, guided by your love-winged messengers.

Tree or person, lightning can topple whatever it hits.
Console us with your truth, God, that trouble,
trauma, tragedy — like lightning — just happen at
random and without malice from you. Should it
strike, we'll look for rainbows, assured of your
presence as we pick up the pieces.

After Loss

Time helps, Lord, but it never quite blunts the
loneliness that loss brings. Thank you for the peace
that is slowly seeping into my pores, allowing me
to live with the unlivable; to bear the unbearable.
Guide and bless my faltering steps down a new
road. Prop me up when I think I can't go it alone;
prod me when I tarry too long in lonely self-pity.
Most of all, Kind Healer, thank you for the gifts of
memory and dreams. The one comforts, the other
beckons — both halves of a healing whole.

Prayer for the Sick

Bring your cool caress to the foreheads of those suffering fever. By your spirit, lift the spirits of the bedridden and give comfort to those in pain. Strengthen all entrusted with the care of the infirm today, and give them renewed energy for their tasks. And remind us all that heaven awaits— where we will all be whole and healthy before you, brothers and sisters forever.

Bless those who tend us when we are ailing
in body, mind, and soul.
They are a gift from you, Great Healer, sent to
accompany us along the scary roads of illness.
Bless their skills, medicines, and bedside manners.
Sustain them as they sustain us,
for they are a channel of your love.

Bless My Doctor

Her hands are so gentle and skilled,
her mind so quick,
her heart so filled with compassion.
Bless her in all her duties,
and in her free time, too.
For she needs physical and spiritual
refreshment these days,
and you, Great Physician, are the one
who can help her the best.

REMIND US, LORD, that you dwell among the lowliest of people. You are the God of the poor, walking with beggars, making your home with the sick and the unemployed. Keep us mindful always that no matter how much we have, our great calling is to depend on you—for everything, every day of our lives.

Let Me Help

Help me to see with new eyes today—especially
the burden of care that others harbor within them.
Grant me insight to see beyond smiling faces into
hearts that hurt. And when I recognize the pain,
Lord, let me reach out.

Grains of Sand

*We are surprised by joy, God of re-creation,
when we see despair outwitted by simple acts of
love as small as grains of sand.*

*Keep us searching, believing, and building
upon them, realizing that grains of sand
make dune, shore, and desert.*

It Is Blessed to Receive, Too

*Being ill lately has been difficult,
having to accept from others all the time.
But you have shown me, good Lord,
that unless I am open to others' gifts,
I deprive them of all the
pleasure of offering.*

Support Group

This is a club no one wants to join, Lord; its membership dues are high: trouble, illness, loss. Bless all who share and support.

Like your loaves and fishes, their courage multiplies and feeds all who come in need.

Finally, I've emerged from the dark night into the light with new energy, renewed vigor, a body that responds again.

Thank you for blessing me with recovery and wholeness.

Reflections of Light

Held up to your light, our broken hearts can become prisms that scatter micro-rainbows on the wall. Our pain is useless as it is, redeeming God, just as a prism is a useless chunk of glass until light passes through it. Remind us that the smallest ray of sun in a shower can create a rainbow. Use our tears as the showers and your love as the sun. Looking up, we see the tiniest arches of hope in the lightening sky.

Please, Comforting Spirit,
show me what it means to let go
the hope that others will be my cure.
You, Great Physician, are my healer
in this quiet hour.

Prayer for Healing Disagreements

We come, needing your help to move beyond
the times we hurt one another and the times
we willingly misunderstand, cherishing our
differences, and the times we assume we know all
there is to know about each other and turn away.

And then there are the times that we make private
rules, only to publicly condemn anyone who fails
to abide by them. We limit one another by labeling,
interpreting, conditioning, insisting, resisting,
defining.

From all this, Lord, we come, asking that you
forgive us as we forgive those others. We need
new eyes to see and new ears to hear. Be with us
as we do so.

Mustard-Seed Progress

O God, healing is going so-o-o slowly, and I am impatient and grumpy. Mind, body, or soul, this could take a long time.

Remind me that recovery is a journey, not a hasty jet-lagged arrival. Bless me with faith to sustain me, step by small step.

You do miraculous things with faith as tiny as mustard seeds that, in time, blossom into awesome growth.

I hold that picture as I make mustard-seed progress along the road to healing.

Healing Memories

How blessed are the good memories, Lord!
In fact, I am beginning to see that
my happiness can consist largely in the looking back.
For that I am thankful, as I lie here, unable for
the moment to be active.

*We are blessed by your enveloping spirit.
Your comfort touches us like gentle rain
and hushed snow.*

Binding Up a Broken World

You created your world as a circle of love, designer
God, a wonderful round globe of beauty. And you
create us still today in circles of love—families,
friendships, communities.

Yet your circle of love is repeatedly broken
because of our love of exclusion. We make separate
circles: inner circle and outer circle; circle of power
and circle of despair; circle of privilege and circle
of deprivation.

We need your healing touch to smooth our sharp
edges. Remind us that only a fully round, hand-
joined circle can move freely as a spinning wheel or
the globe we call home.

Dear God,
you hold a place for me that is
far better than my earthly home.
There I will know no sickness, no pain, no death.
There I will experience your presence.
You love me and will care for me for all eternity.
Bestow on me the courage to believe in my heavenly
home, to believe in your abiding love.
Give me your peace.
Amen.

LORD, I AM GLAD TO BE YOUR CHILD. Thank you for your Holy Spirit, who watches over me. Keep me safe until you come for me, just as you promised. Amen.

The Lord is my shepherd,
I shall not want.
He makes me lie down in green pastures;
he leads me beside still waters;
he restores my soul.
—*Psalm 23:1–3*

Jesus answered them, "Have faith in God. Truly I tell you, if you say to this mountain, 'Be taken up and thrown into the sea,' and if you do not doubt in your heart, but believe that what you say will come to pass, it will be done for you. So I tell you, whatever you ask for in prayer, believe that you have received it, and it will be yours."

—*Mark 11:22–24*

Guard me as the apple of the eye;
hide me in the shadow of your wings.

—*Psalm 17:8*

You have been around since time began, dear God. Help me to know that my life is important to you, that my health and well-being are important to you. Just as Jesus restored sight to the blind, give me eyes to see your will in my life. Heal me of my illnesses, my selfishness, my injuries. Give me your peace. Amen.

Healing Powers

*Thank you, thank you, thank you
for your healing powers.
You have lifted me from my hospital bed
and set me on the road to recovery.
I know it could have gone another way,
and so, before I leave this room,
I want to take a moment to thank you
for your mercy toward me.*

Dear God,
help my unbelief.
When I'm in pain, I forget that
you care about me.
I forget that you have helped me
through other trials.
I forget that you hold me in your arms
to keep me safe.
I forget that you feel the pain I feel.
I forget that you love me.
I forget that I am important to you.
Show me your presence—
let me feel your enveloping love.
Heal my hurting soul.
Thank you for staying with me
even in my unbelief.
Amen.

Give me strength to deal with today's uncertainties.
Give me courage to handle the problems I must face.
Let me feel your presence, Lord, when
I'm not sure if you remember my name.
Let me know that my struggles cause you pain also.
Calm my anxious soul.

HEAL MY HEART TODAY, I pray. I am so lonely. I feel desolate, and it is not my imagination; I really am alone now. Oh, God, be my companion and helper in the days to come. Have mercy on me, I beg you. In Jesus' precious name, amen.

Gratitude Before Healing

Lord, it seems like my own body is turning against me. I pray to you for healing, but first let me thank you for teaching me a new appreciation for my body and the health that until now I took for granted. Let me thank you for showing me that these things are gifts, borrowed from you for only a short time on this earth. Let me praise you for the wonders of your creations, precious and unique, revealing your greatness to the world.

I see that my body is not turning against me, but it is teaching me an important lesson: As I struggle through this illness, I am reminded to love and appreciate your gifts of my body and health, and in so doing extend my love and appreciation to you, my Creator.

I want to be well, Lord.
My heart needs to be freed from its mistrust,
its self-centeredness, its frailties.
Give me courage to face
my fears and faults, my inner soul.
Cleanse my insides so that my body may be healed.
Help me remove the obstacles that
may impede my healing.
Let me be brave enough to face
whatever you have in store for me.
Let me rest in your serenity.
Help me believe in your peace.

Prayer for Acceptance

My body is still sick, dear God. Why? Help me accept your will. If I must be sick of body, please heal my soul, my heart, and my pain.

Show me your strength, that I may be strong. Hold me in your hands, that I may rest knowing your presence. Help me accept what is in store for my body. Let your peace flood my soul. Amen.

Blessings

We notice your presence, Lord,
in a baby's sweet smile, a phone call
from a friend, a flower blooming through
a crack in the wall — all these simple,
beautiful gifts remind us of you and your
great love for us. Fill all our days with
these offerings from your hand, Lord,
and fill our hearts with gratitude for
the small, simple blessings
you give us every day.

Lord,
what a privilege and blessing it is
to live in your grace right now. Because you
promise that I am living in your grace, I can rest
assured that every goal, every dream I will ever have is
already in your hands. My life is enriched, fulfilled,
and illuminated by your marvelous grace for me. It
is an incredible blessing that I can never deserve,
but I will cherish all the days of my life.
In Jesus' name, amen.

I AM BLESSED by your presence, Lord. I saw you today in the smile of a tiny child and in the eyes of an old man I passed on the street. I saw you in the way a hummingbird lingered at my window just long enough to nod its head in my direction, and I saw you in the sunlight that bounced off my desk. Because I saw you today it was a good day, a blessed day, and I thank you.

Blessed Baby, Welcome

*Bless this newborn, Lord, with hunger of soul
and mind to match a growing, thriving body.
At awesome moments like these,
we, your "big children,"
feel your blessing wrapped around us like
a baby's blanket. Give us wisdom,
patience, humor, stamina, humility, joy,
and grace to pass on.*

*Lord,
we ask your blessing on our children today.
When you walked among us, you taught us how
precious these little ones are to you. Please protect
them as they go out into the world, Lord. Send your
guardian angels to keep them from harm and
watch over them as they sleep. We trust them
to your perfect care and ask that you draw
them nearer to you each and every day.
In your name we pray, amen.*

Small Miracles

Bless you, Lord!
The heavens declare your glory;
the skies proclaim your mighty power.
And here I am, looking up into
those vast regions, knowing
that the tiniest cell in my body
is a most glorious miracle as well.
Bless you, Lord!

Our Animal Friends

The creatures we befriend and call our pets add a special dimension to our lives. In them we find our caretaker instincts rising up to nurture and protect. We form bonds of love and loyalty with your creations, God, and we learn to appreciate the traits and distinctions unique to the animal friends we have come to hold dear. Thank you for the joy and comfort they bring. Thank you for blessing us with them.

Creator God,
bless the animals that
you have trusted to our care.
Give us the wisdom to care for them
in a way that would please you,
for we know that they are also the
marvelous work of your hands.
Our pets are faithful day in and
day out and ask so little in return.
Make us aware of the companionship and love
we receive from these creatures of yours,
and show us how you would have us love them.

WE TURN TO YOU, God, before enjoying this meal because we know that you have provided it for us out of the bounty of your goodness. Bless the hands that prepared this food as you bless it to our bodies and us to your service. With each head bowed and each heart praising you, lay your blessing upon us. And as we enjoy all that you have provided for us, we ask your blessing also on those who are hungry or suffering. Amen.

Bless this home, Lord. Please fill every heart that lives here with your peace and joy. Make this a home where others enter gladly, feel welcome and loved, and leave refreshed.

Protect this home from disaster and brokenness, Lord, and make it a shelter in the storm for all those who dwell within.

Bless our going out and our coming in from this day forward, and please accept our praise and thanksgiving for this place we are privileged to call home.

Bless our hearts, Lord,
with an openness to believe fully
in your message of salvation and eternal life.
Thank you for making our acceptance into your
heavenly kingdom as easy as saying, "I believe."
We know you are the giver of faith, hope, and love,
and that there's a reason why faith comes first.
Thank you for making belief in you so simple
and yet so profound. Open our hearts,
Lord, and lead us ever closer to you.
In Jesus' name, amen.

ALMIGHTY GOD, how blessed we are by the seasons you've created. The crisp air and clean snow of winter inspire us, the blossoms of springtime speak to our hearts, and the long days of summer fill us with an appreciation for this world of yours. When fall comes around again, all bathed in golden hues, we don't fear, Lord, for we know the seasons of our lives are as surely in your hands as the seasons we enjoy. Thank you for being a constant presence through every season.

A New Beginning

*What a blessing
to have a second chance!
Grant me the wisdom
to use this opportunity wisely.
And save me from the fear
that I'll fall into the same
old traps as last time.
This is a brand new day,
a whole new beginning.*

Lord, bless your church in this world in which we live. Your true church is made up of all those who believe. We pray for direction from you and that we would always turn to your Word and search your heart in prayer. Honor us with your presence, Lord, as you promised you would whenever two or more are gathered in your name. May all we do bring glory only, always to you.

We come to you today, Lord, to ask you to bless all those who go out of their way to come alongside and help others. In particular, we ask your blessing on the firefighters and police officers who risk their lives each and every day. But we also ask you to bless the doctors, nurses, pastors, and people in every neighborhood who volunteer to make life a little easier for someone else. Smile down upon all those who reach out to others, Lord. In your name we pray, amen.

Respite

*I celebrate the gift of contentment,
knowing there is no guarantee it will last.
But for now, it's great to rest —
just to rest in this wonderful calm.*

BLESS THIS COUNTRY and those whom you have chosen to lead it, God. So often we fear for the future of this land we love. We see the scars of violence and the heartbreak of those who are left in its wake. We see corruption, and we pray for your forgiveness. Please bless us all with your wisdom and discernment, God. Turn the hearts of this country back to you that we might become all you intended for us to be—a light in the world you created.

Freedoms

God, my freedoms are much like the air I breathe; they are taken for granted until they are taken away. So today I want to pause a minute and thank you for the freedoms of all kinds that I have been able to enjoy.

These blessings include being able to freely worship, choosing what I will wear, voting for whomever I wish, deciding whether and whom I will marry, and having the freedom to travel from place to place.

These are just the beginning of a very long list. God, you are the author of freedom, the champion of the privilege of making one's own choices. Help me to honor you today by choosing well and wisely.

God of peace, I thank you for the ways in which you have blessed my life with your harmony. When circumstances have been chaotic, you have extended your calm to my heart. But there are havens where I can find outer peace as well—in trusted friends and family, in places of solitude, in the sanctuary of nature, even in sleep. Bring peace to my world through the peace you have placed within me, and help me not to forfeit that peace, even in times of trouble.

In Good Times

*Bless us in this time
of good fortune.
Give us the grace to be grateful
for newfound comforts,
magnanimous among those
who have less, and
thoroughly giving with all
we've been given. Amen.*

Happiness is a wonderful state of heart and mind, dear God, and I thank you for blessing my life with many happy times and experiences. But I am even more grateful to you for the deep and abiding joy that remains in my spirit, even when the circumstances that make for happiness have evaporated. For even in the most difficult times, Lord, the blessing of your joy can bring a song to my heart, reminding me that your good plan for my life will prevail.

THE GREATEST BLESSING you have bestowed on humankind is your love, and it is from your love that we learn how to love each other. In the context of these loving relationships, we flourish individually and also as a community.

God, thank you for the love you have placed within my life, your own love and the loving ways of others. Help me to pass your love to the hearts of others, so that your legacy of love will carry on in this generation and the next.

The Blessing of Music

From the time I was a child, God, music has played a significant part in my life. It has soothed me, made me dance, helped me learn, entertained me, captured my imagination.

I have never stopped being carried along—from experience to experience and life-stage to life-stage—by my favorite songs. These songs have been my companions, my solace, my dream nudgers.

I have felt the power of music create meaningful moments, bring my family together, and lead me into worship.

It is an awesome and wonderful blessing you have given us—this gift of rhythm, melody, and rhyme we call music. Thank you.

Together

Bless this partnership, God,
the friendship of her and me.
And remind us both:
Every gathering of two
is really a fellowship of three.

You did not create us to be lonely in life, Lord. You said after you created the first man that it was not good for him to be alone. Community is your blessing, your design to alleviate loneliness and isolation. As I look around at the various sources of community you place in my life, I see how you seek to safeguard me from going it alone. My work, my recreation, my place of worship, my family, my friends—all bring the blessing of community to my experience. Thank you for these opportunities to enjoy your gift of sharing life together with others.

Painting, sculpting, dance, music, design, theater, writing—these are just a few of the many evidences of our creative nature. In art, our ideas, perceptions, feelings, interpretations of life, longings, memories—who we are—can be expressed in what we create. Creator God, this passageway from our inner world to the outer world is the blessing of art. By what we create, we reflect your own creative nature. Thank you for sharing this element of yourself with us, for in it we find great joy and fulfillment.

*I praise you for the blue sky,
the comforting breeze, and the rustle of leaves.
Nature is so remarkable. When you created the earth,
you thought of every detail. Every color is so perfect,
each sound so peaceful. The lapping water of the
shoreline lulls me to sleep, the gorgeous sunrise
wakes me in the morning, and the beauty of all
that surrounds me gives me peace during
the day. Thank you for your artistry.
I enjoy it so very much. Amen.*

Let the words of my mouth,
and the meditation of my heart,
be acceptable in thy sight,
O Lord, my strength,
and my redeemer.
—*Psalm 19:14*

Creations

The universe and all it contains put me in awe of your creative ability, God. No matter where I go, no matter what time of day or year, I experience the blessing of your creative genius.

You show it in the things I see: the terrains of the world, from deserts to rainforests; the variety of animals, from puppies to polar bears; and the stars, moon, and sun deep in space. Then there are the tastes, smells, and sounds that fill my experience with pleasure: the sweetness of a nectarine; the fragrance of a rose; the roar of a waterfall.

Sometimes I close my eyes and just enjoy the feeling of grass under my feet and a breeze touching my skin. All is so beautiful and good.

YOU GIVE MY EXISTENCE PURPOSE, God—in the work you call me to do, in the people you ask me to love, in the skills you intend for me to use, in the opportunities that come my way. It's true that I go about my day as one who has a mission to fulfill, and I realize that my mission is this: to do and be the best I can with what you have given me. I accept that mission today as a blessing from you, God, and I thank you for the grace and strength you will provide for me to carry it out.

The rain falls and the sun shines on the good and the bad, Lord. But all things being equal, I am so glad that you have called me into your family. You offer me a purpose and standards, you provide discipline and opportunities. Even one day with you offers more goodness than I could repay. Stand with me forever, please. Amen.

Cheering Section

Bless those who mentor, model,
and cheer me on, Lord,
urging me toward goals I set,
applauding as I reach them,
and encouraging me
to try again when I don't.
Remind me to be a cheerleader.
I say thank you for those
who are mine.

When I think about the ecosystem, I am astounded by your wisdom. Your earth works far better than anything any human could design. It is so hard to fathom your power, but I am grateful that I see it at work every day. Amen.

Lord, let me be a blessing to someone today.

Thank you for the sound of the rain; thank you, too, that it will help our farms to flourish. Tomorrow our grass will be a little greener, our weeds a little taller, and the world will look and smell as though it just had a cleansing shower. Thank you for being God of the rain.

Thank you for the sunrise and the sunset. They are reminders of both your faithfulness in my life and the beauty of your handiwork.

I HAVE SURVIVED A DISASTER, Lord. I am still able to live and to love and to be whole. From this disaster I have learned to appreciate all the blessings around me—like the song of a bird, the smell of a rose, and the grasp of a baby's hand. Thank you for allowing me to live another day and for teaching me about what's really important in life. Amen.

Thank you for giving me the wings to rise above the painful parts of life.

Thank you for teaching me to be content; it certainly saves a lot of time that might be spent complaining. The inner peace that I have is one of the many gifts from you. And the moral strength that you instilled in me has carried me through many otherwise destructive times. You are indeed a God of practicality and love.

*Before I fade into
the welcome arms of sleep,
I want to spend a moment with you,
asking for your blessing—on my
friends and loved ones, on my church
and community, and on myself.
You are a faithful God, strong and true.
I am grateful that you can hear me
morning, noon, and night. Amen.*

I HAVE LEARNED TO BE HAPPY with a little and with a lot. Mostly because you have been there for me whatever my circumstances. Today I stand before you, thankful that my life has come full circle. I look into the eyes of my grandchild, and I know you are God and you are in absolute control. Thank you for my many blessings. Amen.

Sometimes it's easy to believe that winter is a season to endure until springtime ushers in the days of summer. But then, when I step outside on a calm winter's day, I find tiny wonders everywhere, tucked away like special treasures for the one who cares to seek them out. You have made winter as a special season of rest and reflection, Lord, a time of discovering beauty against the backdrop of bleakness. Thank you for the exquisite blessings of winter.

HELP ME, LORD, when my purposefulness is
endangered by my lack of willpower or by the
many demands of my time — there is so much I
want to schedule and incorporate into my life!

Help me see the goal. Help me to keep it in sight
and to be inspired by the thought of reaching it.
Help me not to waste my energies focusing on past
failures. Rather, help me to throw my whole self —
mind, body, and emotions — into gaining the
victory. With your help and blessing, I can win!

Celebration

I love being alive, God!
Thank you for each day of life you
have given me. I am especially grateful
for today, for the moments it contains —
opportunities for me to enjoy blessings of
all kinds. There are many people, places,
and experiences yet to come my way, and
I live in anticipation of these joys and
wonders. I begin celebrating life today
as I live in full awareness of this
priceless gift from your hand.

In Praise of the Usual

So much to celebrate, Lord:
waking to dawn gilding the trees;
squeezing fresh orange juice,
its zest clinging to my hands all day;
making a new friend,
talking to an old one;
watching the first leaf bud,
raking the last.
Each day's turning brings gifts
from you to celebrate.

THESE LIFE EVENTS are wonderful milestones along our way, marking our joys and moments of significance, helping us to remember that you have made our lives rich and full. Thank you for blessing us with yet another year of life. We rejoice now, mindful of your goodness to us.

EACH YEAR WE CELEBRATE this time together.
It is made special by what it recalls and by the
memories we've had along the way as we have
celebrated together with friends and family,
and even those times we have celebrated alone.

We can see that you are doing a new and
blessed thing in our lives, Lord, and we rejoice
in your goodness and love! In the midst of all
the excitement you are creating for us, we pause
to remember you as the source of all things
wonderful. Thank you for new beginnings,
for hearts full of hope, and for the opportunity
to celebrate with you all the blessings you so
graciously bestow upon us. Amen.

Treasured Relationships

For the friends who have remained with me over time, the family that has seen me through the worst, the relationships that have been a significant part of my growing process—for these I give you praise, dear God.

And I rejoice with my whole heart because these have been the most meaningful treasures I have enjoyed in life.

I celebrate them today by asking you to visit each one with a blessing that far surpasses what I've received from them. And if you should choose to bless them in some way through my life, I would be honored.

O come, let us sing to the Lord;
let us make a joyful noise to the
rock of our salvation!

—Psalm 95:1

THE BEAUTY OF OUR EXISTENCE is framed within the beauty of the year's seasons, Creator God. The springtime reminds us of life's beginning, of renewal, of the times we have blossomed in some way. Summer comes, and we see all the brightness, warmth, and growth you bring to our lives.

In the fall we find a relaxed contentedness. In a way, this speaks of maturity that emerges in our lives when we learn to slow our pace and enjoy the blessings right in front of us. And then, as winter brings the end of the cycle of seasons, we warm ourselves by fires, gather family near, and relish precious memories.

God, it is thus we realize that life does not ever truly end, but rather it continues on — in new seasons, in new lives, and, for each of us, in eternity. So we celebrate the seasons with which you bless our world and our lives.

You bring so many wonderful and interesting people my way, God. No two are alike, and I enjoy the uniqueness of each one. Today I want to celebrate the new relationship you have brought to my life and to ask that you bring about your good purposes in and through it. Lead us both in the process of discovering the beauty in one another, and show us how to give and receive the love and respect that must exist to make our relationship a celebration.

Lord,
we lift up our marriage to you
with thanks for the gift you gave us
when you first brought us together. It isn't as fresh
and new as it was when you created it for us, Lord, so
we ask your blessing again. Wrap the life we share in
your protective arms so that the world will never be
able to tear us apart. Fill us anew with the
precious love you gave us for one another,
and hold us firmly in your eternal love.
In Jesus' name, amen.

Happy Anniversary

Thank you, Lord,
for our marriage.
Like a wedding band,
our love encircles but doesn't bind.
Like a vow, our love sustains
because of what the words mean.
In your grace, our love has the
permanence of rock, not of walls,
but of a bridge to moments
ahead as special and bright
as when we first met.

Blessings on the Anniversary Couple

There is no greater mystery than love, Lord of covenants and promises. We are in its presence on this anniversary day.

Bless those who live, day after day after ordinary day, within the fullness of married love, surely one of the greatest mysteries.

Bless them as they honor their past, even while they create a future. Let them bask in the pleasures and applause of today, when we bow before their accomplishments, which, like the rings of growth on trees, are an inspiration and blessing to us all.

ALL OF US LOOK FOR SOMETHING, for someone in whom we can believe. God, today I celebrate that you are trustworthy and that I can choose to trust in you. I celebrate that my faith is rooted in the faithfulness of your character, and I revel in the strong sense of security I feel as I lean steadily into your unconditional, unfailing love for me. My faith rests fearlessly in you because your love is perfect.

Gratitude fills my heart so often
for all you bring to my life, God,
that I cannot help celebrating from time to time.
Today I celebrate the simple blessings in my life.
I ate and drank because you provided.
I slept in safety, sheltered from the
elements because you provided.
I enjoyed the company of others, sharing
conversations and smiles, because you provided.
I am clothed and clean because you provided.
Goodness comes from your hand,
Lord God, and I celebrate
the goodness of all you provide for me.

Wedding Blessing

Bless the couple before you, Lord,
with peace, not of a stagnant pond,
but of deep rivers flowing;
with strength, not of sheltered dogwood,
but of oak, sycamore, and beech,
storm-tossed and rooted;
and with power, not of fists and temper,
but of blooms stretching
toward the sun.

Celebrate Love

May you enjoy all the streams of love
that flow into your life:
the love from family and friends;
the love from parents and children;
the love from pets;
and the love from God.
Celebrate love all day long. For it is the breath
of your existence and the best of all reasons for living.

Hope is one of the most powerful life-giving motivations known to humankind. The tiniest shred of hope gives us great courage and strength to face bleak circumstances and overwhelming odds.

There have been times when I felt as though I would never smile again, but you have whispered the promise of tomorrow in my ear. And hope, far off as it has seemed at times, has never failed to carry me to a place of blessing.

Thank you, God, for the hope that has encouraged my life. Today I can celebrate that hope because it has kept me alive and brought me to this place of joy.

Milestone Birthday

Bless this candlelit festival of birthday celebration, Lord, for our special loved one. Join us as we blow out candles and joke about setting the cake ablaze, about golden ages and silver hairs. Our laughter is bubbling up from gratitude that the years are only enriching this special celebrant. We are grateful that the years are also enriching our lives as friends and family, for we are the ones receiving the best birthday gift today: the gift of knowing this special person.

With boldness and wonder and
expectation, I greet you this morning,
God of sunrise and glistening dew.
Gratefully, I look back to all that was
good yesterday, and, in hope,
I face forward, ready for today.

THE CHILDREN REMIND ME that the challenges of life are to be met with wonder, optimism, and faith, Lord. Children make the most of opportunities to play and enjoy a sunny day. They freely give and receive affection. They pick flowers, sing songs, and say what's really on their minds without undue self-consciousness.

Their curiosity is voracious, and they get a kick out of trying what they have learned. They easily let go of their anger, and they readily forgive. And while their foibles are larger than life, their redeeming qualities are larger still.

I celebrate the children today, God, and the qualities they bring to life that remind me how to remain happy and free.

Our Prayer for Earth

For clean air and pure water; for glorious colors in sky and tree in first and last bloom, in the wings of migrating butterfly, goose, and bird. Lord of all, to you we raise our hymn of grateful praise.

For wildlife sanctuaries, open range, prairies, mountains; for backyard gardens; for cornstalks and bean stems growing tall, then bending low for harvest; for your generous gifts that meet human need. Lord of all, to you we raise our hymn of grateful praise.

Every day and night we marvel at your wondrous care. Constantly you guide our choices, inviting us to creative living.

All creation reflects your empowering love: rolling countryside, stark canyons, majestic mountains, delicate wildflowers, and sturdy roadside blooms. Sunrise and star, warmth and chill all declare your glory, singing together. Lord of all, to you we raise our hymn of grateful praise.

For love that gives us soul-satisfying happiness; for families, friends, and all others around us; for loved ones here and loved ones beyond; for tender, peaceful thoughts. Lord of all, to you we raise our hymn of grateful praise.

Life is good, Lord!
When I see your hand at work,
I just have to stop and celebrate all that you are and
all you have given to the world. Holding a newborn
baby, hearing children at play, receiving a letter from
a friend, seeing the sun dipping down behind the
horizon . . . in moments like these,
I celebrate the life you have given me.
And I thank you. Amen.

First Day of Advent

Connected in memory to holidays past, like links
in a colorful paper chain decorating the tree, we
begin another advent. Some recollections are
happy and pleasant, others sad and empty, yet
each brings us to this new starting point, as fresh
and full of promise as an egg about to hatch. Make
all things new this holiday, even old memories, for
this is the season of second chances.

Every generous act of giving,
with every perfect gift, is from above,
coming down from the Father of lights,
with whom there is no variation
or shadow due to change.
—James 1:17

A Small Prayer While Wrapping Presents

Tangled in tape, lists, and holiday wrap, we are all thumbs with excitement! Bless the surprises we've selected, wrapped, and hidden. Restore us to the joy of anticipation—we want to be surprised, too.

Our wish lists include the gift of possibilities, of ears to hear a summons and eyes to spot another's need or triumph, and of being able to make a difference. As we cut and tape, God of surprises, remind us to keep in touch with the gift's recipient after the wrapping papers are long gone and the ornaments packed.

Grace for Advent

You are a welcome guest at this table, God, as we pause in the midst of this bell-ringing, carol-singing season of too much to do.

Send us your gift of silent nights so that we can hear and know what you will be bringing us this year: yet another gift of hope. Bless our gathering around this table; we will set a place here each day for you.

Join us in our daily feast, for which we now give thanks. May it nourish our busy bodies as the anticipation of your presence among us does our weary spirits.

We're caught up in well-worn, comfy traditions, Lord. Keep them worthy, for like a deer path through the forest, they lead us forward and back. Thank you for the divine love and holiness found in the ordinary.

Blessing for Our Feast

We gather around this feasting table,
humbled by our bounty,
Lord of abundant life; we have
so much more than we need.
We confess that we are poised,
fork in hand, ready to overdo.

Help us learn better how
to live as grateful,
if overstuffed, children —
delighted, surprised, and generous
with the sharing of our good fortune.

Bless us now as we enjoy it amidst
food, friends, and family.
We give the heartiest thanks for
your diligent, steadfast care.

Blessing for a New Year

The slate is clean, Lord, the calendar as bare as the Christmas tree. Bless the New Year that beckons. We sing of you as help in ages past but need to know you as hope for years to come.

Help us face what we must, celebrate every triumph we can, and make changes we need. We're celebrating to the fullest this whistle-blowing, toast-raising moment, for it is the threshold between the old us and the new us.

God, a new year brings a feeling of freshness — I see the possibilities of the future and of discoveries yet to be made. I look forward to stepping into the days ahead, knowing that you will guide me into the good purposes you have planned for my life. I ask you for an extra measure of courage, strength, optimism, and faith to meet every challenge along the way.

Palm Sunday Grace

We gather this day around a table of celebration, shouting welcome and "Hosanna!"

And for us at this table, God of lions and lambs, heal any hurt feelings, saddened hearts, and lonely days so that we can truly celebrate being together this day in a crowd of friends and family. We have a long week ahead before we celebrate again.

Easter Meal Grace

We are celebrating today, O God, a mixture of bunnies hiding colored eggs and angels rolling away stones. Join us as we gather to share a meal and ponder both, enjoying the one and giving thanks for the other.

Bless those at this table savoring the food and the message of this day. Remind us, too, Lord of unexpected appearances, that this also is the season of spring, a time when rebirth is not so surprising after all.

Blessing for a Newborn

Bless this little one of so few days.
May he be prosperous in all his ways.
Healthy in body and mind,
growing strong and kind.
Bless this little one through all his days.

Blessed Teens

This birthday, Lord, my child becomes a teen. Surely it's just the smoke of 13 candles making me cry. But, O Lord, wasn't it just yesterday that there was just a single candle?

From before that day to this, I've trusted you. I ask you now to bless the youthful drive to risk making choices; the struggle to be heard; the changing body, moods, and mind. Bless—and this is hardest for me to say—the urge for independence.

Bless me with ears to listen, a shoulder to lean on, and the good sense to build bridges, not walls.

Blessing for Grandparents

They've added a new holiday, Lord, a day to honor the grandparents who tended us so well. Pause with us as we play again in the dusty lanes of childhood at Grandma and Grandpa's house. Bless these bigger-than-life companions who helped us bridge home and away, childhood and maturity. In their footsteps, we made the journey. Thank you for such a heritage and a day on which to express our gratitude.

Longtime friendship is a two-way mirror, O God, a gift from you that returns our best selves reflected in the joy others get from just having us around. Thank you for the gift of perseverance that keeps old friendships new.

Celebrate!
I am forgiven!
The conflict is over.
The animosity long forgotten.
How wonderful to be set free from rancor.
How good to have a friend
instead of an enemy.
How beautiful our renewed friendship.
I am forgiven!
Celebrate!

He Is There

Know the benediction of the Lord in these days! In all your comings and goings, know he is there. In all your joys and triumphs, know he upholds you. In all your worries and heartaches, know that he cares. And in all your worship, celebrating, dancing, laughing—wherever you are—know that he is pleased.

Celebrate the Word!

May you rejoice in the written Word.
The Scriptures can come alive for you;
only take, and read.
Discover the acts of God in history.
Travel with his disciples along
the pathway of service.
See how his church began,
how it grew
down through the centuries.
Yes, celebrate the written Word,
for it is a mirror of,
and a witness to,
the Living Word of the heavens.

Lord,
I'm having another birthday.
I forget when I got to be old.
It seems like yesterday I was celebrating the big "1-0."
Then it was the big "4-0." Now, it's ... well, you know
what it is. I don't feel any different, except maybe a
whole lot smarter. Thank you for every day and
for every year. Thank you for those who wish to
celebrate with me. Lord, you provide a very
good life to those who love you.
Amen, and amen.

MY HEART IS JUMPING FOR JOY as I sit here in this pew. I see so many young faces looking earnestly for you in the words and songs. I rest in knowing that your spirit is strong and far-reaching ... and it endures forever. A life touched today is a life touched for a lifetime. This is pretty exciting stuff, God. Thank you for allowing me to be a part of it. Amen.

Different Is Lovely

We want to belong, and we go to great lengths to
fit quietly in, forgetting we are like snowflakes, no
two, thank God, alike. Each snowflake and child of
yours is the same in essence but different in form.
Bless our unique, one-of-a-kind value. We are
heartened to know that no one is created more
special. It is not your way to be unnatural, to
make one snowflake better than another.

*I will celebrate your love
every day of my life.*

Father God,
you have blessed me with yet another
new year in which to grow. I have more
opportunities ahead of me in which to find
the potential you have placed within my life.
Thank you for each of the past years, for in them you
have taught me how to embrace truth and nurture
love. I can't count the number of times I've returned
to your wellspring of wisdom to gain insight
and understanding for my life. Thank you for
your guidance. Please lead me into today
with an open heart and mind,
ready to learn still more.

I thank you that you have answered me
and have become my salvation.
The stone that the builders rejected
has become the chief cornerstone.
This is the Lord's doing;
it is marvelous in our eyes.
This is the day that the Lord has made;
let us rejoice and be glad in it.
—Psalm 118:21–24

My body, my mind, my emotions, my spirit. God, I celebrate the capacity you have given me in each of these parts of myself. Sometimes I may focus on what I lack because I see others enjoying what I wish I had. But today I want to rejoice in all that I do have, in all that gives me pleasure and makes me unique. You are an incredible Creator, and I praise your skill as it is revealed in my body, abilities, feelings—all of my being.

I bless the Lord who gives me counsel;
in the night also my heart instructs me.
I keep the Lord always before me;
because he is at my right hand,
I shall not be moved.
Therefore my heart is glad,
and my soul rejoices;
my body also rests secure.
For you do not give me up to Sheol,
or let your faithful one see the Pit.
You show me the path of life.
In your presence there is fullness of joy;
in your right hand are pleasures
forevermore.

—*Psalm 16:7–11*

Message of Giggles

Bless the children, God of little ones, with
their giggles and wide-eyed awe, their awaking
assumption that today will be chock-full of
surprises, learning, and love. Neither missing
nor wasting a minute, children take nothing for
granted, a message that blesses us. We will go
and do likewise.

Rejoice, the Lord is King!
Your Lord and King adore;
Mortals, give thanks and sing,
And triumph evermore:
Lift up your heart, lift up your voice;
Rejoice, again, I say rejoice.

—*Charles Wesley,* Hymns for our Lord's Resurrection

For Joy of the Seasons

It's snowing. I celebrate the snowmen
soon to be built by happy children.
It's raining. I celebrate the seeds
that will soon be flowers.
It's sunny. I celebrate the warmth on
the happy people playing in the sun.
It's cold and crisp. I celebrate the crunching leaves
under the feet of schoolchildren.
I celebrate all the seasons, Lord;
each gives us its special gifts and joys.

I CELEBRATE MY RELATIONSHIP with you today, Lord. I have often looked and not found you, but I was looking in the wrong places. You were always where you were supposed to be—deep inside my heart, waiting to give me your peace. You have been there during my joyful moments and in my darkest minutes. You've stood beside me when I've felt shamed and humiliated; you've given me strength when I needed courage. I celebrate you today, Lord. I celebrate you!

The Biggest Gifts

I have no big event to celebrate today, Lord. But I think I'll celebrate anyway. You've given me a job, a house, a wonderful child, a hardworking husband, and so much more.

Today I'll celebrate the dirty laundry because my family has clothes to wear; I'll celebrate the dishes in the sink because my family is fed; I'll celebrate the mess in my child's room because he has toys and a place to call his own.

There is so much to celebrate—when I just look at what I've been given. The smallest things in life are actually my largest gifts from you! Thank you.

My soul makes its boast to the Lord;
let the humble hear and be glad.
O magnify the Lord with me,
and let us exalt his name together.

—Psalm 34:2–3

Topical Prayer Index